BE! LIVE!

Constance Roslinda Gary

Copyright © 2018 by Constance Roslinda Gary.

All rights reserved. No part of this publication may be reproduced, distributed, or transmitted in any form or by any means, including photocopying, recording, or other electronic or mechanical methods, without the prior written permission of the author, except in the case of brief quotations embodied in critical reviews and certain other noncommercial uses permitted by copyright law.

Except otherwise stated, all scripture is taken from the King James Version of the Holy Bible (Public Domain)

Any people depicted in stock imagery provided by Pixabay and Pexels are models, and such images are being used for illustrative purposes only.

Reprint edition 2018

Printed in the United States of America

ISBN: Paperback: 978-1-949362-27-5
        eBook: 978-1-949362-26-8

Library of Congress Control Number: 2018952046

Stonewall Press
363 Paladium Court
Owings Mills, MD 21117
www.stonewallpress.com
1-888-334-0980

CONTENTS

BECAUSE YOU COME TO ME	1
BELOVED MOMMA	3
BREAD OF LIFE	6
DEDICATION! DETERMINATION!	7
ENFORCED IDLENESS	8
FOR IT IS WRITTEN	10
FROM NOW ON	13
GO FORTH	14
HIDDEN ONE	16
HOUSE OF BONDAGE	18
I FORGIVE	20
IT'S YOU KNOW WHO	22
KILLING FIELDS	24
KING VALIANT	26
KINGS OF CITIES	28
LIVING MEMORY OF LOVED ONES	30
LOVE LOCKED UP INSIDE	31
MY BLESSED REDEEMER	32
MY PLEASURE	36
NEW WAVE OF MY HEALING!	38
OUTCRY FROM SILENT LIPS	39
REACH THE UNREACHABLE	40
SOAKING IN JESUS' LOVE	42
TRIBUTE TO A GREAT MAYOR	44
VISION	46

WHAT NOW MY BROTHERS & MY SISTERS?	47
WHAT'S THE PRICE OF FREEDOM?	49
WITH THE HELP OF GOD ALMIGHTY	51
YOU BLESS US!	53

Because you come to Me! Come!
I AM drawing you near to Me
Come! I will in no wise cast you out! (John 6:37)
Behold ! The lamb of GOD
"Who takes away the sins of the world (John 1:29)
Lo! I come quickly! (Psalms 37:1)
Fret not yourselves because of evil doers (Psalms 37:1)
Faint not at the promises of GOD..." (Galatians 6:9)
In these last & evil days…. Many have turned away…" (Timothy 3:1)

From the love of GOD many have turned away
From the love of GOD many have gone astray!
Yes, Son! My prized disciples are ensnared!
Entangled in the web of sin!
Perversions! Secret hidden sins!
Ministering at MY Holy altars!
My blood can't rest! Shocking!
Abominations in My temples! Houses of worship!
I will provide a sacrificial center!
Where priest, who are the apple of My eye
Will minister to My sheep & shepherds
Who have gone astray!

I AM Holy! Be ye Holy! (I Peter 1:16)
I will seek you out!
Churches are shamelessly lukewarm!
My anger burns hot within Me!

But My mercy is everlasting!
REPENT! *"Kingdom of GOD is at hand.."*
Turn from your wicked ways!
Pray! Humble yourselves!

I will hear from heaven
Heal your land! (Your temple, body)
Lay before ME! Soak in ME!
Lay before ME! Soak in ME!

"I AM the LORD GOD that health thee" as only I can! (Ex. 15:26)
REPENT! Turn
From your evil ways!
"For I come quickly!" (Rev. 22:12)
REPENT! REPENT!

Set up a soaking center!
It's an ark of safety as in the day of Noah!
Before the wrath & judgment of GOD!
Is released!

Soak in ME! Seek MY face!
Seek My face daily!
Not just weekly/biweekly
Praise GOD!

Hear My voice!
Obey!
Do all that I say!
Tell the people!

Feed My sheep!
In soaking centers!
A new wave of healing!
Hallelujah! Amen!

BELOVED MOMMA

You loved all five of us
Different textures, colors hues
A collection of egos & temperaments
A human collage

You coasted along life's highway
A victim of many battles & wars
You turned into an outstanding lady
Yet remained basically as you are

All this talk about degrees & sororities
All mumbling about professions/careers
All this pomp & circumstance
Where are you going anyhow?

Angelic messengers sent
Now I'm going to give Holy Ghost
Wait a minute! That's absurd!
People will think I'm mentally disturbed

You sought ways to feed us
Keep us one group
Your life was tough
We robbed you of your youth

You surrendered totally to JESUS
During one of your hospital episodes
At a new dawn you considered
Where would I have gone yesterday?

You sat in bed really considering
Putting as all kidding
To Hell, no matter all good deeds
JESUS CHRIST! Come into my heart!

Well, nevertheless! It's OK!
Going to meet my Master today
Fill me completely! Cleansed with
Blood of JESUS! Filled with Holy Ghost!

Cleanse me from all unrighteousness
Who cares about another test
Don't you see JESUS standing there
Don't fret or worry I AM here

Come to Me without stretched hands
You are going with me to My kingdom
Yes! There are many mansions there!
Leave this one with worries/cares! (2x)

Get up out of that body
Come with Me!
There are loved ones
Waiting for thee!

Slowly! Quietly! Release!
From the snared body
Released! Now free!
To step into eternity! Hallelujah!

With freedom in my wings
I fly toward heavenly throne
With CHRIST JESUS at my side
I see the face of GOD this day

Don't cry or groan!
Don't be sad or moan
I've gone to a glorious place!
To be saved is no disgrace

With JESUS in my heart to stay
I see God's face today Goodbye!
I soared in clouds so high
Your birth into eternity is nigh!

Are you really ready to go
This one thing I know
Be careful in your choices
Be not deceived by demon voices!

Consider you ways
Consider receiving CHRIST today
Consider the time
Say to JESUS! Your will not mine!

This is not sad or even bad
Do not feel sorry for me or be sad
Look up! Live!
For I took my Master's hand!

I stepped from mortality
Into immortality
Oh! Death! Where is your sting?
Oh! Grave! Where is your victory?

Satan! Get Thee hence!
GOD! My Father reached out
Touched me! I'm no longer the same!
Be saved, baptized, filled in JESUS' Name

Glory! Glory! Glory! Hallelujah! (4x) Praise GOD!
Gospel of preparation of peace
Go out teach and reach! Sing and shout!
LORD! Thank You for this child, who didn't cry or pout!
But went about doing her Father's will

Thank GOD with much love I remember still
Those quiet cool nights of hopelessness
When soft hands would touch my body
And ask me to LORD JESUS CHRIST confess

JESUS! Forgive me of my sins	Hallelujah! glory to GOD!
LORD JESUS! Let me start again	Gospel of peace of preparation
LORD JESUS! Forgive my foolish ways	Your feet are shod
LORD JESUS! Come into my heart	As down well trodden paths today!

Do not be afraid!	Run swiftly the race with patience
LORD GOD is on your side	Keep the faith!
Do not stumble and fall!	Steadfast! Unmovable!
JESUS CHRIST is LORD of all!	JESUS, The author & finisher!

Hallelujah! (3X) Amen
Reach out! Touch someone!
To receive JESUS! Be born again!
Don't grow weary, tired or distress!
Get up with JESUS each day & do your best!
Hallelujah! (3x) Praise GOD!
Hallelujah! (3x) Thank the LORD!
Hallelujah! (3x) Praise GOD!
Hallelujah! (3x) Thank You GOD!

Amen! Amen!
World without end Amen! Amen!
Hallelujah! I love you, Baby! I want you to always remember that!
Oceans of heavenly love,
Momma   Praise GOD

Sent the living Bread of Life! (John 6:31)
The Holy ONE! The supreme sacrifice!
Died and arose up from the grave! (John 6:50)
He's 1st! Believe on HIM! Neither hunger nor thirst!

GOD sent His SON to do His Will!
"Not My will", said JESUS, *"but Thy Will!"* (Luke 22:42)
So those who believe on JESUS gain eternal life!
Bread from heaven! JESUS! JESUS CHRIST!
Hallelujah! Amen!

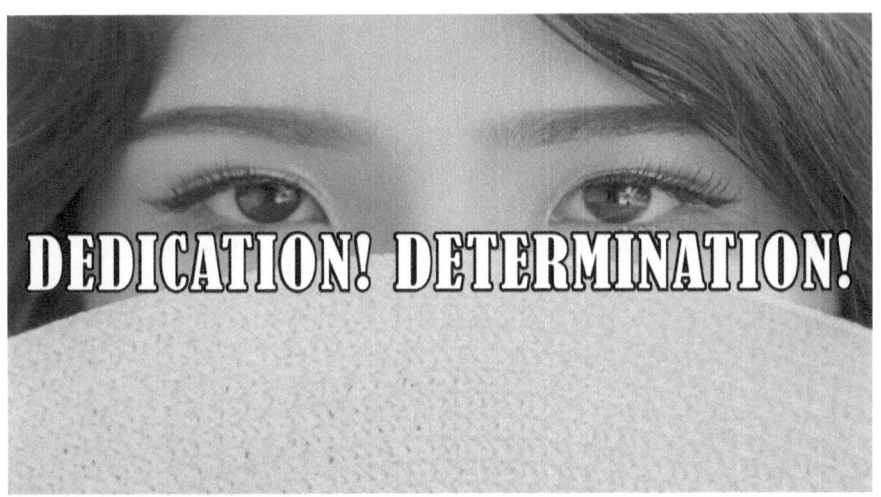

DEDICATION! DETERMINATION!

You are joy & inspiration
You are a flower flowing with dedication
Dedication to beautiful goals in life
Determination to become excellence in life
Of course, there are many other goals
But this one must be told
You have succeed in becoming a beautiful young lady
An excellent first born baby
Because of you my life cycle feels complete
There are many trophies at my feet
There's joy & feelings of well being
I have accomplished my mission as a human being
Be fruitful & multiply
Such strange words indeed
Yes! Be fruitful & multiply
That is commanded from on high
Love you so much! Miss you more!
Remember walk through every opened door
May GOD continue to bless the works of your hands
And quickly unite you & your earthly god man.
Love! Peace! Prosperity! Life everlasting! Joy!
Patience! Long suffering! Loving kindness!
All praises be unto GOD!
Your FATHER! Your provider! Amen! Amen!

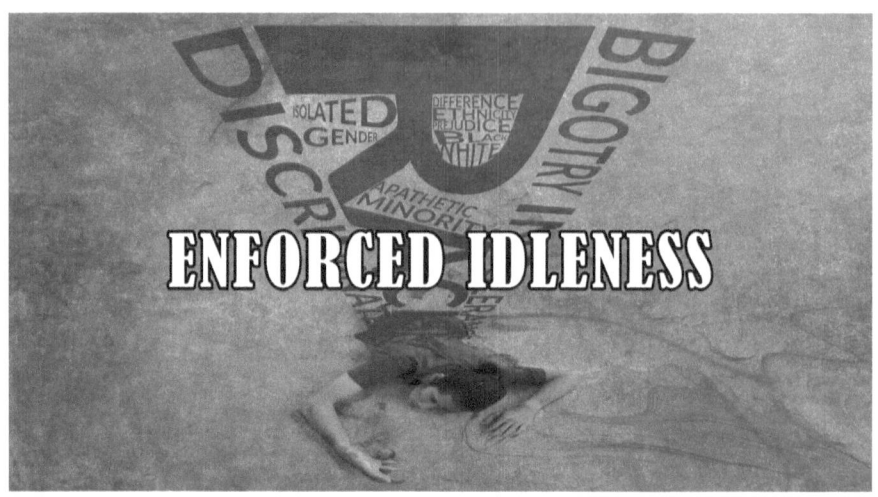

(12/1/86)

Slave minimum wages/ prisoner's labor

Today's new form of slavery is slave minimum wages system. Slave idleness! This is the state of being forced through economic oppression into impoverish living standards. The lack of adequate good paying jobs often drives many in training jobs in order to collect welfare dole. This meager money is measured out bi-weekly or monthly. In most cases it barely cover the rent and hardly pays incidental utilities and other living expenses. Welfare limit choices of where you live, go to school and ultimate goals in life.

- It becomes a dull thud in your life
- It blocks creativity.
- It destroys families.
- It kills ambitions
- It maims thinking processes.

The emancipation mechanism is career oriented courses designed for the individual to be grafted into highly skilled, upward mobile, superior paying positions. Minimum wages is not enough. Part time fast food position do not enhance economic development. We, the people, need relief from ever increasing crimes, foreclosures, homelessness, homicides, mental illness, suicides.

We, the people, need collaborative corporate and institutions strategies implementation of success generated upwardly mobile positions.

We, the people, must break this treadmill cycle of chronic unemployment.

We, the people, must break free from this charade of enslaved, forced idleness.

We, the people. Realize when one is enslaved… all are affected, because this of priceless input from one valuable human being.

"For there is no respect of person with GOD" (Romans 2:11)

Set us free! Don't hire to fire! Hire to inspire! Hire to acquire dignity and independence!

FOR IT IS WRITTEN

For it is written
"Cursed is …who hangs on a tree"
CHRIST died for you and me
To set us free

For it is written
"Cursed is … who hangs on a tree"
CHRIST suffered and died
To set you and me free

For it is written
"Cursed is … who hangs on a tree"
CHRIST! Sanctified was crucified
Died on the cross for you and me

For it is written
"Cursed is …who hangs on a tree"
CHRIST! "It is finished!" He cried!
CHRIST was crucified and died

For it is written
"Cursed is …who hangs on a tree"
39 stripes whipped upon His back
Healing every sickness and disease

For it is written
"Cursed is …who hangs on a tree"
Yes! CHRIST was crucified
To set us free

For it is written
"Cursed is … who hangs on a tree"
CHRIST, Son of the living GOD
Died to set us free

For it is written
"Cursed is… who hangs on a tree"
My Savior! CHRIST was crucified
On that cursed tree, HE died!

For it is written
"Cursed is … who hangs on a tree"
CHRIST JESUS of Nazareth died
On the cross, He was crucified!

For it is written
"Cursed is …who hangs on a tree"
He was made a curse for us
He was wounded, scourged, crucified

For it is written
"Cursed is ... who hangs on a tree"   (Galatians 3:13)
"My GOD! My GOD! Why hast Thou forsaken Me?" (Psalms 22:1)
CHRIST was crucified to set us free!

For it is written
"Cursed is... who hangs on a tree" (Galatians 3:13)
"FATHER into Thy hands I commit My Spirit" (Luke 23:46)
Freely I lay down My life! I give it!

For it is written
"Cursed is ... who hangs on a tree" (Galatians 3:13)
"For this purpose was the Son of Man manifested to destroy the works of the devil" (I John 3:8)

Nails driven into His hands & feet
Cross lifted up! Heaven & earth did meet!
He opened not His mouth like a sheep
GOD of Israel does not slumber nor sleep

He look across all eternity
He shed His precious blood
For you and me
GOD! FATHER! Look from above

Angels, heavenly hosts
Disciples looked in disbelief
Mary and Mary Magdalene
Cried out in utter grief

What a lesson this Calvary
What demonstration of GOD's love
"For GOD so loved the world
He gave His only begotten Son..." (John 3:16-17)

To suffer and die on Calvary
"That whosoever believe on Him
Shall not perish, but have power!
Everlasting life" (John 3:16-17)

GOD! Thank You for Your beloved Son!
GOD! Thank You His precious shed blood
GOD! Thank You for Your resurrection
GOD! Thank You for salvation hour!

Now! It's time to give your heart
To give your heart to JESUS!
You don't have much time!
LORD JESUS! Come into my heart

Forgive me of my sins
Save me! Help me to begin again!
Redeem me from lost time!
Set me free from the evil one!

CHRIST JESUS! My risen LORD!   Hallelujah! Hallelujah!
Take control of my life!   Hallelujah! Praise GOD!
Have Your way, LORD JESUS!   Hallelujah! Hallelujah!
Come into my heart, today!   Hallelujah! Praise GOD!

"With the gospel of peace of preparation   *Lions gird with the Spirit of truth*
My feet are now shod   *Feet shod with the gospel of preparation*
"Putting on the full armor of GOD   *Sword of the Spirit to quench*
"Helmet of salvation, breastplate of righteousness   *Every fiery dark of the enemy"*

…we wrestle not against flesh and blood
But against principalities of spiritual
Wickedness in high places
For the pulling down of a strongholds (Ephesians 6:11-18)

"Let this mind be in you, which is CHRIST JESUS" (Philippians 2:5)
"Let the peace of GOD rest, rule, abide among you
Hence forth and forever more" (Colossians 3:15-17)

"Put on the mind of CHRIST JESUS
Having done all stand" Just stand! (Ephesians 6:13)
"Let this mind be in your,
Which is CHRIST JESUS…" (Philippians 2:5-7)

"Whatsoever you bind on earth
Is bound in heaven
Whatever so is loose on earth
Is loosed in heaven…" (Matthew 18:18)

Hallelujah!!! Amen!
Hallelujah! Praise GOD!
Hallelujah!! Amen
Hallelujah! Praise the LORD! AMEN!

From now on!
He is with you unto the end!
He is here and now!
JESUS is my eternal friend!

I have life!
I have peace!
I will not perish!
I have everlasting life!

Lay aside all malice! All guile
Hypocrisies, envies, all evil speaking (I Peter 2:1)
Yield yourself to the LORD
Let Him live through you!

GO FORTH

GO forth! Preach! Teach! Reach!
Thus saith the spirit of GOD!
Take no thought of tomorrow!
Take no second thoughts

Get your house in order!
"Be not afraid! Neither be dismayed!
"For lo I AM with you even unto the
Unto the ends of the earth..." (Matthew 28:20)

Put not your confidence in man (Psalms 146:3)
Be not deceived… (Galatians 6:7)
Be not weary of well doing…. (Galatians 6:9)
Believe on the LORD JESUS CHRIST
And ye shall be saved.. (Acts 16:31)

Saved from iniquity, foolishness,
Wandering, wondering, worries
Released them all to ME now
In the name of JESUS!

Surrender fully to Me during
Time of fasting & praying
Your sins are forgiven!
In the name of JESUS!

Though they be as scarlet as blood Because of the blood of JESUS
They will be as white as snow! Repeat! Though they are as scarlet as blood
They are as white as snow! Believe on ME only

Seek My face more diligently daily! A great task is in store for you!
You will travel extensively! You & M………..!
Do not look to yourself, your own understanding for answers!

Do not question My Will any longer! Trust & obey! Trust & obey!
"Seek first the kingdom of GOD and all its righteousness and all else shall be added unto you…" (Matthews 6:33)

Pray! Watch out for more trouble! But I, Your LORD GOD shall sustain you. Abstain more from foolish talking & idle words! I your LORD GOD shall hold you accountable for every stray word. A word not in line with My word. Speak My word!

I AM the way, the truth, the light no man can come unto Me except through My resurrected Son CHRIST JESUS! Take My word! Feed My sheep! If you love Me feed My sheep!

Amen! Amen!

HIDDEN ONE

My beloved son
You're the hidden one
My beloved daughter
You're my hidden one!

My son! My daughter!
My most beloved ones
You loved me unconditionally
You loved me completely

While I tried to get myself together
You embraced! We are sister & brother!
You stood by your Mother
You held on to one another

Come out from among them
Stand up in the sun!
Come out! Sing a hymn!
Stand up my daughter

My beloved child!
My beloved one!
My love child!
You stood by me while

Thank you for Your love!
Thank you for your push & shove
Thank You pulled me thro' many cold nights
You pulled me out cold sweet frights!

Thank you! Thank you, my beloved one!
Because of you, my new life begun!
You're a landmark moment!
You were a bright comet!
In my life I saw me in You!
In my life you showed me what to do!
In my struggles I became calm
You were peace in the middle of my emotional storms!

Thank You! Thank You! Thank You!   Thank You! Thank You! Thank You!
My beloved One!   My Beloved One!
Live on! Laugh!   Live on! Laugh!
Your life has just begun!   Your life has just begun!

Love You! Love You! Love You! Love You! Love You! Love YOU! Love You!
Thank You!
Praise GOD for you
Bless your Mother too! Amen! Amen!

(1/9/87 4:30am)
Many women and children are daily being sentenced to a life of poverty in court systems. There crime of getting pregnant culminating with the birth of a live child by an irresponsible father. She is shortly thereafter abandoned, separated from the father of that offspring.

The court system then is approached by that woman with child/children seeking child support. She is most cases may or may not have proper sensitive representation to plea her cause. The court system must pass judgment based on lawyer, legal representation which may or may not be her favorable circumstances. The results of these hearing are often times inadequate child support and/or a life sentence to impoverishes.

- Poverty like death has no color line or social stratification.
- What are the contributing factors to such consistent inconsistencies?
- Why do the borderline indigent remain so?
- Why do so many mothers walk into court hopeful and leave disillusioned?
- Why are two-thirds of the children in this affluent country face a life of poverty, hunger and potential homelessness?
- Why are welfare roles swelling with cast off's, the children, and cast asides, their mothers.
- Why must human beings be sentenced to such degradation?

- Why must mothers be made ashamed of motherhood through the welfare subsistence?
- Why should her children be sub-nurtured and malnourished?
- Why should she be casually denied adequate housing due to economic deprivation?
- Why are countless former wives with your children, your sisters, even your mothers live in houses of bondage, poverty?

We must stop the abandonment of our future generations, our children and grand children!
GOD bless America!

I FORGIVE

"Behold, I come quickly…" Hark! "Behold, I come quickly…" (Rev. 22:7)
"And behold, I come quickly…" (Rev 22:12)

I forgive those who have offended me!
You have forgiven me of countless offenses!
"Against You and You alone have I sinned…" (Ps.51:4)
And done these things in Your sight!

Forgive me, LORD, as I forgive all!
All those who have offended me
Throughout my life from its inception
Yes! LORD 5x Change not chance

Hallelujah! To the Lamb of GOD!
JESUS! Our soon coming KING!
"Fear not, my little flock…" (Luke 12:32)
Lamb of GOD who was slain…foundations…

"Yes! I come quickly for a church
Without spot or wrinkle." (Eph.5:27)
Ask me to make you spotless & wrinkled free
As only I can do this miraculous inner healing

Washing you with hyssop! Whiter than snow!
No one can ever love you like I do!
"…I will never leave you or forsake you."(Heb. 13:5)
"Behold! I come quickly…" (Rev 22"7)

Do the works of a chosen disciple
Do not be discourage or afraid!
Do the greater works
Work the creative miracles

I will heal the broken hearted	Hallelujah! Glory to GOD!
Sustain the weak, feeble, downtrodden!	Hallelujah! Praise GOD!
Raise the dead	Thank You! JESUS
Set the captive free!	Praise GOD! 7x70 Amen!

IT'S YOU KNOW WHO

It's you know who
From you know where
Lots of people, too
Should have been there

Some were in denial
Others still on trial
Some turned him in
Others were fake friends

Some used crack
Others react
Some are x-rated
Others overrated

What's your philosophy?
I'm on bended knee
Will somebody, please?
Come! Help me!

Running sacred & free
Don't let them catch me
Here come the cops
My stomach's in knots

Some ran the other way
Others wouldn't play
Some said, "Not today!"
Others looked away

Some are on fringes
Others knew the truth
Some became unhinged
Others were troubled youth

Some numb pain
Others snort cocaine
Some use legal pills
Other addictive thrills

Fired! Terminated!
Job situation ill fated!
Standing in free meal lines
I know how it feels

Locked up in jail cells!
Closed up in cubical
Locked up in institutions
Caught up in prostitution

Had it in the bank
IRA Investments
Stocks Bonds Tank
Now embarrassment

Long unemployment lines
Crying all night at times
Waking to another day
Don't know what to say

If I can make it
Minutes! Hours! Days!
Keep it in check!
My mind is a wreck!

Maybe I'm depressed!
No, maybe stressed!
Better, yet just upset!
I can do something I'll regret!

I feel like getting strung out
On my favorite pain killer!
Like going over the top!
Gotta resist addiction thriller!

Monster can't take dominion over me
Submit to GOD! Resist! Devil must flee!
GOD only you know!
JESUS! Save me! GOD! Help me!

Every temptation, adversity
Only You can help me!
Turn this financial tsunami
Only You can rescue me!

Clean me up!
Fill my cup!
Sanctify!
Satisfy!

My problems –eradicate!
My emotions-sedate!
My finances- restore!
Open and/or close doors!

Great GOD Almighty!
My soon coming KING!
JESUS! My Savior! My Friend!
JESUS! My lover until the end!

Come into my heart today!
You're welcome to stay!
Forgive me of all my sins!
Help me to begin again!

JESUS! Save me, today!
Welcome in to stay!
Forgive me! I pray!
Teach me Your way!

LORD! I love You!
LORD! I need You!
LORD! I praise You!
LORD! I thank You!

Show me! Way! Truth! Light!
You can make everything alright!
You can heal the broken heart!
Lead me to a brand new start!

Thank You JESES! Hallelujah!
Thank You JESUS! Praise GOD!
Thank You, JESUS! Hallelujah!
Thank You, JESUS! All praises do to You!

So BE it! AMEN!

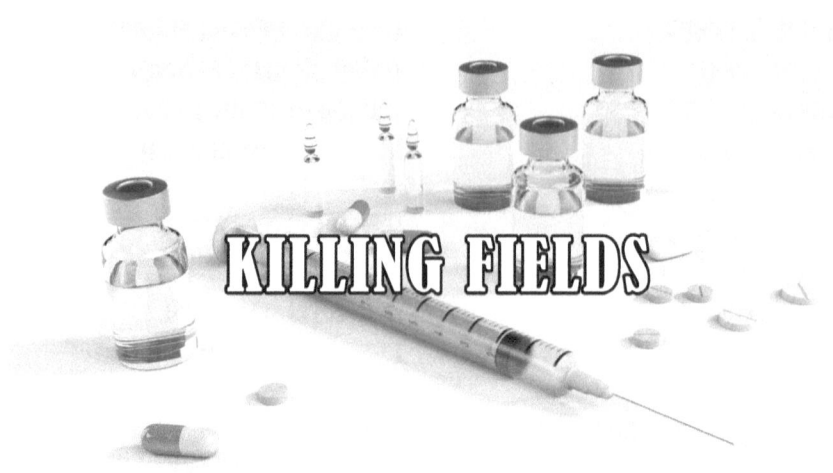

KILLING FIELDS

What did she die of?
Pull the plug!
Oh! Not just heart trouble!
Cause of death! Broken heart!

Oh! Yeah! It's cheaper!
Than to keep her!
Can't afford to maintain life!
So we'll chose death!

It certainly is because
Anyone can get tired of you
And say off with his/her head
I mean! Pull the Plug!

What was the condition again?
Recite the long tedious ailment list
It's summed up in three words
Pull the Plug! Pull the plug!

Shut down all systems
Close all doors & escape hatches
Notify nurses, nurses' aides
Play the game! Pull the Plug!

What new term is that?
It's simple! Family members
Talk with Dr. and decided
To "PTP" No hope! No point!

Some choice!
Some choice words!
Pull the Plug!
Sounds like death to me!

How cold, gruesome, unkind!
Its plain, simple murder!
They sit in a neat row at
Funerals that they didn't have to go

"PTP" of hope in life!
"PTP" of dignity & self-worth!
"PTP" of desire to live!
"PTP" of love!

Isn't this fun! Guess what?
Your trouble has just begun!
You should be tried for murder
Condemned guilty! Serving time!

Murder is murder! That's all to it!   *"Vengeance is mine, saith the LORD...*
There's nothing polite or intellectual   *I will repay..." (Romans 12:19)*
Murder is murder! Your Mother or Father?   *"Vengeance is mine, saith the LORD..*
Your spouse or loved ones?   *I will repay..." (Romans 12:19*

KING VALIANT

(11/87) 9:45am

This is a tribute to a fallen leader! This is in honor of King Valiant 1st
Stricken with heartaches, cares & woes! Who sought a high political post!
This is an eulogy to a champion greeter! Who saw a political machine at its worst!
Who challenge & conquered many foes! Who fought for his city the most!

This is to you! King Valiant! A native Chicagoan!
Yes! You were the King of Chicago! Slain by stressful situations!
Yes! You are still alive in our hearts! A native son! Whose 2nd tenure
Yes! You are still well loved! In office had just begun!

Yes! We will remember your winning smile!
Yes! We will remember you charisma & charms
Yes! We will remember your antics so wild!
Yes! We will remember your outstretched arms!
Yes! We admire you inner strength! You, now, fallen before us lain
Yes! We realize the fortitude! So unexpectedly! Gone so quickly!
Yes! We acknowledge your persistence! However we will remember!
Appreciate tough love from your pours exude! As we trod steadily forward!

To wave that victory banner!
In honor of your gregarious manner!
Used effectively to get a tough job done!
"Well done, my beloved, son!"

So much to do!
So much left undone!
Rest, dearly beloved!
The victory is won

KINGS OF CITIES

(1 Kings 3:9-13)

You are Kings of cities
Appointed! Anointed! Ordained!
You are rulers over many!
You were not just elected, but selected!

Seek GOD's wisdom!
His gifts of discernment & understanding!
Seek GOD's guidance! His kingdom!
Love the LORD with all your heart!

We need GOD every hour!
With Your blessings we are showered!
"Seek first the kingdom of GOD…" (Matthew 6:33)
"Gospel of preparation …feet shod." (Eph. 6:15)

Hallelujah! Praise GOD!

Seek GOD's approval and nod!
Seek to go before His throne!
Cry out, "Have mercy on us, LORD!"
Desire to hear Him say, *"Well done!" (Matthew 25:23)*

Strive to do GOD's will
Others will say GOD is with him still!
Seek to do things pleasing in GOD's sight!
To love GOD with all your mind & might!

Hallelujah! Praise GOD!
Hallelujah! Praise the LORD!
Hallelujah! Thank You, JESUS!
Hallelujah! Glory to GOD!

"...with the gospel of the preparation of peace our feet are shod..." (Eph. 6:15)

Hallelujah! Praise GOD!	In still in us Thy wise heart!
Hallelujah! Praise the LORD!	Grant us Thy understanding!
Thank You, LORD!	Give us Thy grace start!
Empower us GOD with Your Word!	Supply us with Thy upholding!

Prove us with Thy judgments!	Praise the LORD! Praise! GOD!
Provide us Thy patience, long suffering!	Praise You, JESUS!
Release discernment!	Hallelujah! LORD!
Send Thy empowerment!	Amen! Amen!

Thank You, JESUS!	
Thank You, LORD!	
Praise You, JESUS!	
Praise GOD! Amen! Amen!	Glory to GOD! Amen!

In living memory of loved ones
Who are imprisoned in nursing homes
And hospice by loved ones
Stripped of their dignity & honor

Countless unnamed millions
Loved ones deemed them to
Cumbersome to keep at home
Too expensive: long term care

In spite of rebellious actions
In spite of loud protests
They sit silently in institutions
And cry openly inside

Oh! GOD! What happened to
Our conscious? Our family?
Our compassion? Our love?
Oh! GOD! Forgive us!

Why march them off to concentration
Camps! Dehumanization!
Demoralization! Extreme negligence!
For mass extermination

Let us go home to die in dignity!
At home with friends & loved ones!
Give us back our clothes & shoes!
Release us! Take us back home!

Death is no threat!
Institutionalization against our wills!
Is a cruel form of living death until
We embrace our "Freedom at Last!"

Thank GOD for Freedom
Great GOD Almighty!
Free at Last!
Free at Last!

Love locked up
Such a deep pain inside
Love locked up
Feelings that must not be denied
Love locked up
What to do?
Love incarcerated
Love between you & me
I love you!
Such simple words
So undenialblely true
Only shown by words

Love is what love does
What to do to show your love
Heaven sent is all love
Help us show more love from above. Amen!

MY BLESSED REDEEMER

When you pathway is dark	I AM the Light!
When lies fly all about you	I AM the Truth!
When your mind is cluttered	I AM the Way!
When your voice is silenced	Shout! Hallelujah!

When your destiny is dashed	I AM the Way!
When your day seemed crashed	I AM the Truth!
When your dreams are shattered	I AM the Light!
When you just can't cope	Shout! Hallelujah!

When life's storm are roaring	*MBR! The great I AM!
When you don't know where you're going	*MBR! I AM the Way!
When your day seems cloudy, blue	*MBR! I AM the Light!
When you don't know what to do	*MBR I AM that I AM!

When you gather your druther	*MBR! I AM the Truth!
When wrong words you utter	*MBR! The warrior!
When you seek a way out	*MBR! Manager babe!
When you scream silent shout	*MBR! Faithful; and True!

When all's well seems lost	*MBR! We behold the lamb!
When you're fired by your boss	*MBR! We see heavenly throne!
When your best friend isn't enough	*MBR! We see Your precious face!
When living seems so tough	*MBR! We look into eternity

When you get up & want to give up　　*MBR! We see sacred gaze from the cross
When your loved one says, "Shut up!"　*MBR! That gaze that saw you and me!
When your alcohol and pains kick in　　*MBR! As You thought upon that cross
When to your perverted thrills you give in　*MBR! I died so to save the lost!
When you race to do wrong　　　　　　JESUS, the most high
When you feel so all alone　　　　　　　JESUS, the most Holy One
When your friends don't understand　　JESUS, the only begotten Son
When you feel less than a man　　　　　JESUS, the sent One

When chaos is your daily bread　　　　JESUS shed His precious blood
When you rather die instead　　　　　　JESUS bled and died
When past grieves you overtake　　　　JESUS with nails driven into His hands
When life's events almost break　　　　JESUS pierced bleeding side

---

When grief & despair you greet　　　　JESUS in You we abide
When you can't go another step　　　　JESUS because of You we're alive
When your enemies you defeat　　　　　JESUS, alive forever more
When your place you didn't keep　　　　JESUS, lives in eternity

When old friends reappear　　　　　　JESUS, You set us free
When loved ones disappear　　　　　　JESUS from hell's grave
When out comes old fears　　　　　　　JESUS from the fiery pit
When demons whisper in your ear　　　JESUS from in hell's abyss

When it seems like you can't go on　　Yes! Your Redeemer is at hand
When you don't have a happy home　　Look up! Laugh! Live young man
When your sweet one is gone　　　　　Look up! Give a shout!
When you're so all alone　　　　　　　My blessed Redeemer brought me out!

When you enforce new rules　　　　　Yes! My blessed Redeemer is here
When you make up new regulations　　Yes! My blessed Redeemer is near!
When you're greeted by old tools　　　My blessed Redeemer, only dear friend
When you hear the same old fools　　　My blessed Redeemer helped me again

When you have seen & heard enough	Look up! Laugh!
When people steal your stuff	Look up! Live!
When addicts tamper with your addiction	Look up high!
When your past is future prediction	Your Redeemer is nigh!

When loved ones disappear	We now sit in heavenly places
When new ones ignite fears	As our beloved One
When catastrophes last for hours	We behold our heavenly home
When promises turn into showers	We behold our heavenly FATHER

When callous madness increases	Yes! Your Redeemer is at hand!
When peace of mind decreases	Look up! Laugh! Live!
When rowdy lewdness abounds`	Look up! Give a shout!
When no one else is around	My Redeemer brought me out!

When life's transitions falter	Yes! My Redeemer is here!
When trouble drives you to altar	Yes! My Redeemer is hear!
When praises fill your lips	Yes! My Redeemer! My dear friend!
When secret sins cause you back slip	Yes! My Redeemer help me again!

When slipping into darkness is not fun	My beloved Redeemer is here!
When you know you are the only one	My beloved Redeemer, what shall I fear?
When you see there's no one to blame	My beloved Redeemer! My provost!
When they won't just called your name	My beloved Redeemer! My lover! My Host!

When callousness& calamities cease	*MBR! My Holy Ghost friend!
When you just fall on your knees	*MBR! My sweet Amen!
When everyone has turned away!	*MBR! My nearest kin!
When you don't know what to pray	*MBR! My JESUS! I'm born again

My Blessed Redeemer! The Master's Plan
My Blessed Redeemer! My Rock! My Stand!
My Blessed Redeemer! My hiding place!
My Blessed Redeemer! My amazing grace!

My Blessed Redeemer! My High Tower!
My Blessed Redeemer! Glory hour!
My Blessed Redeemer! My precious Savior!
My Blessed Redeemer! Alpha and Omega!

My Blessed Redeemer! My dear friend!
My Blessed Redeemer! Be Born Again!
My Blessed Redeemer! KING of Kings!
My blessed Redeemer! LORD of Lords!

My Blessed Redeemer! Prince of Peace!
My Blessed Redeemer! Rose of Sharon!
My Blessed Redeemer! Bright and morning star!
My Blessed Redeemer! Ancient of Days!

From the beginning of time
Throughout all eternity
Today if you chose
You may be free!

Harden not you hearts! Only believe!
This is your salvation to receive!
Step with me into eternity!
Say, "Yes!" to ME! Be free! (Repeat three times)

Hallelujah! Anyhow! Praise GOD! Thank You JESUS! Hallelujah! Glory to GOD! Praise You, JESUS!
Hallelujah! Thank You, LORD! Glory to GOD! Praise You, JESUS! Thank You, LORD! Hallelujah!

Thank You, LORD! Praise GOD! Praise You, JESUS! Amen! Amen!

MY PLEASURE

My pleasure begins & ends with you
My joy is not your toy
My love is from heaven above
Yes! You are my beloved

I need you!
You need me!
You know
Let's go

My heart is not made to ache
Your time is not to forsake
Your love covers me
From head to toe

To a new land
It started in Eden
It's a new Canaan
Let's begin again

It started with Adam
It began with Eve
It was so strange
In the garden of Eden

All called human!
Man and woman
So hard to believe
Magnificently conceived

In passion consumed
It's love at 1st sight
Be fruitful resumed
It's so right

Our love is right
Hold me tight
It's the perfect will
Do you love me still?

Our love is older
With intensive desire
Our bodies smolder
In amber fires

Our hearts beat as one
The way it all begun
Our hearts shall beat
Until in eternity we met

Yes! Loved from head to toe
A glorious feeling, you know
Pure! Undaunted love flow!
Without you where would I go?

Complete love is splendid thing
As vibrant as the birth of spring
As exciting as a new toy
I love you so much, boy!

Sent from GOD!
Thank the LORD!
Heaven never seen
No in between!

Hot passion!
Love not lust!
Pure love! Just
Just because…

It was deemed so
One thing you must know
Love Is sent from above
As it's intended to be

You for me
Me for you
So in love
What to do

Look deeply into
One another's eyes
Touch finger tips
What a surprise

Watching in awe
Splendor arises
Body silhouettes
Against skies

Clasped hands
Walking hand and hand
Talking in quiet whispers
Speaking without words

Joint plans
Man and woman
Silky sighs
Single sign

On one accord
Thank the LORD!
Far off places
Familiar faces

One plus one
Equals one
Leave and cleave
We've one just begun

AMEN! AMEN!

A NEW WAVE OF My healing!
Healing in My wings!
Get ready for a new wave of healing!
Miracles unlike ever seen before!

"Eyes have not seen nor ears heard
Things which the LORD has in store..." (I Cor. 2:9)
Walk in righteousness!
Do the greater work!

Do the works that I give you
With all your might! Be not afraid!
"Fear not for I, your LORD GOD,
Will uphold you with outstretched arms!" (Isaiah 41:10)

Hallelujah! Praise GOD! Hallelujah!
Praise GOD! Praise You JESUS! Thank You!
Hallelujah! Amen! So be it according to Your Will!

Amen!

OUTCRY FROM SILENT LIPS

An outcry from silent lips
An outcry from helplessness
An outpouring of distress
Grief thro' another test

Put your hand in GOD's
And leave it there
Don't retreat or flinch
Put on a new man thro' CHRIST JESUS

Old things are past away
"Behold all things are now new." (II Cor. 5:17)
Be renewed with mind of CHRIST JESUS
That is resurrected CHRIST

Do not look back twice
Do not think about former things
Move forward with CHRIST
All will be well!

Well done! My beloved one!
Well done! My beloved Son!
Amen!

REACH THE UNREACHABLE

Advise the unadvisable
Connect with the unconnectable
Contest the uncontestable
Embrace the un embrace able

Forgive the unforgiveable
Forge the unforgeable
Force the enforceable
Fight the un fight able

Greet the un greet able
Know the unknowable
Like the unlikeable
Meet the unmeet able

Reach the unreachable
Teach the unteachable
Treat the untreatable
Touch the untouchable

Advise the unadvisable
Connect with the disconnected
Sacrifice the unbelievable
Strive with adversity

Oh! GOD of the universe
Creator of everything
Knower of all things
We worship and adore You!

We bow down before You
Thy face we seek
Take not Your Holy Spirit
Restore the joy of our salvation

Creator of all creations
Maker of all made things
Author! Finisher!
Beginning! The End!

Intention of the intent
Contender against contenders
Commander of all commanders
Chief and High Priest!

Almighty and everlasting GOD!
KING of all Kings!
LORD of all Lords!
We praise & magnify Your Holy Name!

YHWH - Shammah	YHWH - Shalom
YHWH - Ra-ah	YHWH - Yireh
YHWH - Rapha	YHWH - Nissi

The sacrificed One	LORD of the universe
Mary's beloved one	Maker of heaven and earth
Joseph's love one	Conquer of hell and the grave
GOD's begotten SON	Over comer of devil perverse

Perverters of the Word of GOD!
Perverters of the purpose of our LORD!
Perverters of message of the living Word!
Perverters of the love of GOD!

"In the last and evil days…
Many hearts shall wax cold
Lovers of themselves and not of GOD…" (II Tim.3:1-3)
"Deceivers, liars, workers of all manner of evil
Turning away from natural use of bodies
Women lusts burning for women
Men working all manner of unseemingly
With their lust burning for one another…" (Rm.1:24-32)

Lovers of themselves and not of GOD!
Oh! Great GOD of heaven!
Hear our prayers of repentance!
Hearken unto our cries for pity and mercy!

I love you with an everlasting love!
Love eternal! Love immeasurable!
Love immersed! Love incredible!
Love indefinable! Love unconditional!

So awesome! So insurmountable!
So passionate! So profane, promising!
Fulfilled with compassion!
Compressed with compassion!

Wait! Again I say wait on ME!
Hear, My voice! "Obey My Word! Do My Will!"
In season! Out of season!
Come close for I AM coming soon!"

Your love is calling Me back!
Your prayers, faith and trust in ME!
Longs for the spirit of truth, the comforter
To rest, rule in your heart richly!

Oh! GOD! My strength, my Holy Redeemer!

I hear You, LORD! I feel You, sweet JESUS!
I will obey and trust! Hallelujah! My LORD!
Not my will but Thy Will! (70 x 7) Amen

This poem reflects the career of the first black popular mayor of the New England states.

This capitalizes year of observing Mayor Thurman Milner of Hartford, Connecticut.

Mayor Milner interacted with mayors at National Conference of Black Mayors and five mayors from Beijing, Peking, and three other provinces.

Best wishes to you in your future endeavors Mayor Thurman Milner. Thank you for touching many lives and being a beacon of hope!

TRIBUTE TO A GREAT MAYOR

Tribute To A Great Mayor
This is a tribute to a great mayor
Who realized it was GOD's will
To serve people made by GOD

A tribute to someone
Many expected failure
Few believe he'd succeed
None understood his impact

Tribute to a man of vision
Who tried to do his best
Bringing public outcry
High infant death, drugs

Who stood for all peoples
Who still does; Believes
King's Dream is not dead
Who ran for Mayoral office

Tribute to a great man
Who didn't sit idly by
Rolled up his sleeves
Stepped into arena

Tribute to a young boy
Who wore hand me downs
Ran down Hartford streets
Now rides in limosines

Destroyers of human fiber
City is 'cause people are
Who marched in parade
Parades for justice

Who trod congressional halls
Who sat in legislative seats
Diplomats greet with smiles
Rub shoulders common man

Just an ordinary man
Flesh, blood & mud
Mud slings of critics
Mud of political cynics'

Three cheers for man of valor
Three cheers 1st New England color
Three cheers honor his Mother
Three cheers cherished by many

Three cheers for a man who stood to the occasion
Saying, "I promise to uphold this office
And represent the down trodden!"
Well done, my beloved son, my beloved one

Well done! AMEN! AMEN!

White hair, deep pool blue eyes! Big tears rolling down CHRIST JESUS' face!
Priorities are so wrong! Time is short! My heart is grieved
So many people have put priorities in the wrong order!
Souls are in the balance! Billions! Billions are being poured into brick and mortar buildings!
Not interested in saving souls. Not interested in temples not built with hands!
Souls are being lost!
JESUS weeps over North America!
Heaven and earth shall pass away! (Matt 24:35)
Seven Billion Souls Crusade
As sands in the dune.

Dear JESUS!

Come into my heart! Take away all sin!
I believe You are the risen CHRIST!
Wash me in Your precious blood!
Write my name in the Lamb's book of life!
Give me the Holy Spirit!
In JESUS' name! Amen!

Shout! Hallelujah! Raise your hands!
Amen!

WHAT NOW MY BROTHERS & MY SISTERS?

What now my brothers & sisters?
Our brother closed his eyes in death!
Opened them in eternity!
Only we are left!

As taps blows!
As tears flows!
As relatives & friends gather!
As family stands together!

As we hug & kiss!
As we remeninish!
As we say our last goodbye!
As we look to the sky!

As we smile & laugh!
As bow heads & clasp hands!
As we consider the past!
As we look to the future!

As he smiles so sweetly!
We already miss him sincerely!
In death dressed so neatly!
Wife, sons & daughters loved dearly!

As we stare vacantly!
As we gazed!
As we examine
As we stammer!

As we mumble words!
As we stumble in herds!
As look into each others eyes!
As we cry & cry!

As we pray to die in our sleep!
As we seek perfect peace!
With a smile on our faces!
As we leave this earthly place!

Just as our Mommy & Daddy!
Just as Grandmothers & Grandfathers!
Just as our ancient ones, ancestors!
Raced towards the sun!

Just as brothers & sisters, if only I could!
Just as we hoped they would!
When I finally fold my hands!
If our legacy will stand!

As we leave our sons & daughters!
Grands & great grands
As we our heavenly home
As some fell left alone!

There is no more pain or sorrow!
We seek answers for tomorrow
We seek 1st kingdom of heaven
Reach the complete number 7

As we wonder have we done our best!
As we ask did we past the test?
Test of time!
Our destiny reached!

JESUS' message preached!
Is JESUS' truly mine!
Our lessons learned!
Our journey sojourned!

Oh! Heavenly Father forgive
Our sins again!
"Against You and You alone have I sinned..." (Ps.51:4)
Done wicked things in thought, word & deeds

I am His
He wipes always all tears!
He is the Alpha & Omega!
He is my personal Savior!

Help us not to offend!
Help us no to pretend!
Help us to love one another!
Help us to give to our brothers!

Help us to love & honor You!
Help us to do what we need to do!
Help us to embrace one another!
Help us seek You like no other!
Hallelujah! Hallelujah!

Have mercy on us!
Forgive us!
Free us!
Save us! Greet us!

Amen! Amen!

Yet profound way
Yes! Listen intently!
Embrace each word!

Caress each episode
In the thrill
Enthralled

Entangled bodies
Interwoven booties
Sweet kisses
Soft hisses

Oooooh's! Aaaah!
Silent screams!
Unspoken words
Billions of touches

Secret glances!
Deep romances!
Groaning groans!
Moaning moans!

Set fires to more touches!
Fluttering nerve endings!
Heart beats skipping!
Emotions flipping!

Body surfing!
Booties slapping!
Body kicking!
Booty licking!

Booties willing!
Thrill giving!
Passions glowing!
Fantasies soaring!

Smile that smile!
Stay for awhile!
Explicit sex demo!
Increase the tempo!

Stare! Don't blink!
Dance in synch!
Booties we uncover!
What a lover!

Grab! Hold me tight!
With all you might!
Create hot desire!
Fire! Fire! Fire!

Reach our peak!
Let booties speak!
At a feverish pitch!
I'll be your bitch!

Secrets kept
Secretions sweat!
Into orgasms slip!
As spasms rip!

A man created to please!
A man free & at ease!
A man with a plan!
A man made for woman!

A man made by GOD!
Husband with a pure heart!
Fathered children with pride!
Man takes everything in stride!

Bathe me in your love!
Baptize me in your juices!
Soothe me with your love!
Smother me with your kisses

How edible!
How incredible!
How detectable!
How exceptional!

Come! Explosively!
Come! Deliciously!
Come! Deliriously!
Come in a deluge!

You're no little boy!
Your woman isn't a toy!
You are a treasure!
Filled with much pleasure!

Strive to attain!
Stroll thro' life!
Survive trails!
Secure your destiny!

WITH THE HELP OF GOD ALMIGHTY

You will hear & do all that I tell you to do!
With the help of GOD Almighty!
With an outstretched hand I will lead you!
With eyes of compassion I will guide you!

With fierce armor I will protect you!
With wings of eagles I will protect you!
With legs of a panther I will race you!
With hinds feet I will elevate you!

With horns & bugles I will announce you!
With sounding brass I will pronounce you!
With loving hands I will caress you!
With strong arms I will hold you!

With steadfast love I will uphold you!
With fiery wall I will shield you!
With longing heart I will draw you near!
With locked feet I will establish you!

With shield of faith I will instruct you!
With bright & morning star I will show you!
With psalms & harp I will console you!
With clashing cymbals I will greet you!

With long life I will satisfy you!
With plenty I will fill you!
With outstretched arms I will engulf you!
With poetry I will lead you into all truth!

With everlasting blessings I will overshadow you!
With everlasting love I will enfold you!
With truth & light I will impregnate you!
With exceeding joy will abound you

With words of my mouth I will delight you!
With living waters I will overflow you!
With Holy Ghost I will fill you!
With power from on high I will replenish you!

Press down, shaken together I will bless you!
With miracles I will astound you!
With signs & wonders I will enlighten you!
With new waves of healing I will empower you!

My footsteps you will follow!
My voice you will hear crystal clear!
My works you will do & not falter!
My grace you will be upheld!

The works I do, you will do!
The words I say, you will say!
The healings I do, you will do!
The holiness I lived, you will live!

The life I give, you will give!
The lessons I taught, you will teach!
The peoples of the world you will reach!
My love for you is bountiful & everlasting!

I give you beauty for ashes!!
I give you joy for all your mourning!
I give you peace that surpasses all human understanding!
Great is My faithfulness to you!

Hallelujah! Praise GOD!
Hallelujah! Praise You LORD!
Hallelujah! Praise You JESUS!

Our soon coming KING!

Where sin dost abound! My grace abounds! (Romans 5:20)
Go! Sin no more! (John 8:11)
"Repent for the kingdom of God is at hand..." (Matt. 3:2)
"No weapon formed against you shall prosper..." (Isaiah 54:17)
"You will keep him in perfect peace... Keep your eyes stayed on Me!" (Isaiah 26:3-4)
"My peace I give to you not as the world gives..." (John 14:27)
"Peace that surpasses all human understanding..." (Philippians 4:7)
"Lo, I come quickly..." (Rev. 22:12)
"Fret not Thyself because of evil doers neither be afraid..." (Psalms 37:1-4)
"In My Father's house are many mansions if it were not so I would have told you so..." (John 14:2)
"Be not afraid..." (Proverbs 3:25-26)
"Greater works than these shall he do" (John 14:11)
"So let it be done according to Your word..." (Matt. 9:29)

LORD JESUS! Soon coming KING! Amen & Amen!

GOD! Thanks Your many blessings!
You bless whether we deserve it or not
You bless whether we're ready or not
You bless 10 fold! No 100 fold!

You bless! 7x
You listen for us to say yes!
You lift! 7x
Your Son a sacrificed gift

You bless us beyond measure!
You bless with silver, gold treasure
You bless us until we're astounded!
You bless as hell's hound !

You bless us in bottomless pits
You bless our sins remit
You bless as world shouts curse & die!
You bless we've no tears left to cry!

You bless & give us victory!
You bless & smile triumphantly!
You bless as friends/family curse
You bless! Holy Ghost us nurse!

You bless us without end!
You bless as strangers we befriend!
You bless our journeys in foreign lands!
You bless with outstretched hands!

You bless when we don't obey!
You bless in church stop all play!
You bless us when we get serious!
You bless us until we're delirious!

You bless! 7x
We confess! 7x
You whip! 7x
When we slip! 7X

You are so gracious & kind
You are a friend to mankind!
You are Alpha and Omega!
You are incomprehensible Savior!

You are end without end!
You are free from all sin!
You are without spot or blemish!
You are where sin is relinquished

You are my friend!
You are where born again!
You are where I want to be!
You are creator of eternity

You are the food we eat!
You are the air we breathe!
You are the water we drink!
You are in thoughts we think!

You are the architect of our bodies!
You are the keeper of spirits!
You are the end of our life's goals!
You are solver of our problems!

You are the constructor of minds!
You are the contractor of time!
You are creator of land, sea & skies!
You are worthy of our tithes!

You're maker of sun, moon, stars!
You flung planets set a far!
You're the author of universes!
You're the beginning of sun burst!

You're the voice in the wind!
You're the ears for all sins!
You're the rider on the tides!
You're conscious to our cries!

You're painter of the universe!
You're present at each new birth!
You're the origin of everything
You're the reason birds sing!

I thank you for blessings untold!
We thank you as our salvation unfolds!
We acknowledge You as the Way!
We accept You in our hearts to stay!

We're inspired by Your Word!
We're acquired thro' JESUS' blood!
We're entranced thro' prophesy!
We're reborn to be free!

We're still in Your will!
We are Yours until!
We're enslaved to Your heart!
We're willing to do our part!

We're obedient to Your voice!
We're dedicated JESUS is our choice!
We're consecrated on Holy ground!
We're tuned to Your voice's sound!

www.ingramcontent.com/pod-product-compliance
Lightning Source LLC
Chambersburg PA
CBHW030104100526
44591CB00008B/264